# Chemtastrophe!

# Kitchen Chemistry

Withdrawn

## Jon Eben Field

Crabtree Publishing Company
www.crabtreebooks.com

# Crabtree Publishing Company
www.crabtreebooks.com

**Publishing plan research and development:**

Sean Charlebois, Reagan Miller
Crabtree Publishing Company

**Developed and Produced by:** Plan B Book Packagers

**Editorial director:** Ellen Rodger

**Art director:** Rosie Gowsell-Pattison

**Glossary and index:** David Pula

**Project coordinator:** Kathy Middleton

**Editor:** Adrianna Morganelli

**Proofreader:** Crystal Sikkens

**Prepress technician and production coordinator:**

Margaret Amy Salter

**Print coordinator:** Katherine Berti


**Special thanks to experimenters Lakme and Owen**

**Photographs:** Title page: Laurence Gough/Shutterstock Inc.; p.2 : Tuskegee University Archives/Museum/Wikimedia Commons; p. 3: Teacept/Shutterstock Inc.; p. 4: corepics/ Shutterstock Inc.; p. 5: (bottom) Jacek Chabraszewski/ Shutterstock Inc., (top)Denis Nata/ Shutterstock Inc.; p. 6: (top) Michele Pringle/Shutterstock Inc., (bottom) Andrea Crisante/ Shutterstock Inc., (middle) Yellow J/Shutterstock Inc.; p. 7: (left) Vartanov Anatoly/Shutterstock Inc., (right) Doroshin Oleg/ Shutterstock Inc., (bottom) Tuskegee University Archives/ Museum/Wikimedia Commons; p. 8-9: Laurence Gough/ Shutterstock Inc.; p. 10: (bottom) Stephanie Frey/Shutterstock Inc., (top) ZTS/Shutterstock Inc.; p. 11: (top) Marek Uliasz/ Shutterstock Inc., (bottom) Tuskegee University Archives/ Museum/ Wikimedia Commons; p. 12: Elena Elisseeva/ Shutterstock Inc.; p. 13: V. J. Matthew/Shutterstock Inc.; p. 14: (top) Peter G/Shutterstock Inc., (bottom) Gos Photo Design/ Shutterstock Inc.; p.15: Olga Utlyakova/ Shutterstock Inc.; p. 16: (top) Gunnar Pippel/Shutterstock Inc., (bottom) Tuskegee University Archives/Museum/Wikimedia Commons; p. 17: (bottom) Kaarsten/Shutterstock Inc., (top) Multiart/Shutterstock Inc.; p. 18-19: Laurence Gough/Shutterstock Inc.; p. 20-23: Jim Chernishenko; p. 24: Blinow 61/Shutterstock Inc.; p. 25: (top) Aspen RockX/Shutterstock Inc., (bottom) Tuskegee University Archives/ Museum/Wikimedia Commons; p. 26: (middle) Karin Hildebrand Lau/Shutterstock Inc., (right) Valentyn Volkov/ Shutterstock Inc., (left) Matka Wariatka/Shutterstock Inc.; p. 27: (top) Lisey Kina/Shutterstock Inc., (bottom) Tuskegee University Archives/ Museum/Wikimedia Commons; p. 28: (bottom) Richard Thornton/ Shutterstock Inc., (top) VR Photos/Shutterstock Inc.; p. 29: Otokimus/ Shutterstock Inc.;p. 30-31: Teacept/Shutterstock Inc.

"How we know" boxes feature an image of American agricultural scientist George Washington Carver. Best known for his research into crop production to help poor farmers, he also created a number of synthetic products used in the home, including cosmetics, bleach, dyes, paints, and shampoo.

**Library and Archives Canada Cataloguing in Publication**

Field, Jon Eben, 1975-
    Kitchen chemistry / Jon Eben Field.

(Chemtastrophe!)
Includes index.
Issued also in electronic format.
ISBN 978-0-7787-5286-8 (bound).--ISBN 978-0-7787-5303-2 (pbk.)

    1. Food--Composition--Juvenile literature. 2. Food--
Analysis--Juvenile literature.  3. Chemistry--Experiments--
Juvenile literature.  I. Title.  II. Series: Chemtastrophe!

TX541.F53 2011          j664          C2010-906582-4

**Library of Congress Cataloging-in-Publication Data**

Field, Jon Eben.
  Kitchen chemistry / Jon Eben Field.
       p. cm. -- (Chemtastrophe!)
  Includes index.
  ISBN 978-0-7787-5303-2 (pbk. : alk. paper) -- ISBN 978-0-7787-5286-8
(reinforced library binding : alk. paper) -- ISBN 978-1-4271-9611-8
(electronic pdf.)
  1.  Food--Composition--Juvenile literature. 2.  Chemistry, Technical--
Juvenile literature. 3.  Chemistry--Experiments--Juvenile literature.  I. Title.
II. Series.

  TX541.F485 2011
  664--dc22
                                                              2010042064

# Crabtree Publishing Company

www.crabtreebooks.com          1-800-387-7650

Printed in China/012011/GW20101014

**Published in Canada**
**Crabtree Publishing**
616 Welland Ave.
St. Catharines, ON
L2M 5V6

**Published in the United States**
**Crabtree Publishing**
PMB 59051
350 Fifth Avenue, 59th Floor
New York, New York 10118

**Published in the United Kingdom**
**Crabtree Publishing**
Maritime House
Basin Road North, Hove
BN41 1WR

**Published in Australia**
**Crabtree Publishing**
386 Mt. Alexander Rd.
Ascot Vale (Melbourne)
VIC 3032

# Contents

# Science and Discovery

**Have you ever wanted to perform your own experiments? You could buy a chemistry kit... or you could also use your kitchen as your very own chemistry lab.**

## Explore and Experiment

A kitchen is a treasure trove of materials that can be used to do simple or complex experiments. Almost every task done in a normal kitchen involves the science of chemistry from cooking to cleaning. Common kitchen materials such as baking soda, vinegar, yeast, eggs, flour, and milk, are used by cooks to perform simple chemical **reactions**, known as cooking or baking. Instead of beakers and Bunsen burners, the standard materials of a chemistry lab, your kitchen has glasses, frying pans, pots, bowls, and measuring spoons. All of them can be used to do simple experiments.

Chefs and chemists deal with matter.

## What is Science?

Scientific knowledge is used every day to develop new technology, solve problems, and create many modern conveniences. Science is based on experiments that are repeatable and produce the same results. Sometimes, scientists happen upon great discoveries through serendipity, which means "lucky accident." They may do an experiment hoping for one outcome and come across something brilliant. Chemistry is a specific branch of science that is concerned with matter. Matter is everything that occupies space and has **mass**.

# Kitchen Chemistry?

Chemists use the term kitchen chemistry to describe "hobby chemistry" or "chemistry done at home." Kitchen chemistry is based on ideas and theories tested in the home laboratory of your kitchen. A kitchen is home to thousands of chemicals undergoing changes in the course of a regular day. Whether you are cooking, baking, or mixing in the kitchen, you use chemical properties to create appetizing meals and snacks. How oil and vinegar are mixed in a salad dressing is chemistry. The softness of a loaf of bread also depends on chemistry. The taste of sugar or salt on your tongue happen because of chemistry. Cleaning up after an experiment uses chemicals such as soap, detergents, and other cleaners.

Bread texture and bubbles are a function of chemistry.

Making donuts is an exercise in chemistry.

## fun fact

Serendipity, or lucky accidents, have meant great leaps forward in science. In 1953, for example, a scientist who was trying to make a hard covering for his car accidentally created plastic wrap.

# Understanding Matter

Matter is in everything around us. The food you ate for lunch is matter. Everything from your desk at school, to this book in your hands, to your eyes, are all made of matter. If you can see it, touch it, taste it, or smell it, it is made of matter.

## Atom Action

Matter is made of atoms. Democritus, a Greek **philosopher** who lived 2,500 years ago, was the first to give atoms a name. Scientists could not prove they actually existed until the 1900s. In the ancient Greek language, atom means something indivisible. Atoms are tiny structures that cannot be seen by the naked eye. They are the building blocks of everything on Earth and in most of the universe.

Without oxygen, water, and sugar, there would be no cake, chocolate chip cookies, brownies, or so many other delicious treats.

## Molecule Motion

Molecules are **particles** that are made up of two or more atoms held together by a **bond**. In the oxygen molecules we breathe, two oxygen atoms bond together, and is known by the chemical name $O_2$. Water is made of two hydrogen atoms bonded to one oxygen atom. It's chemical name is $H_2O$. Other molecules can contain many atoms and be very complex. Glucose is a sugar that has six carbon atoms, twelve hydrogen atoms, and six oxygen atoms bonded together ($C_6H_{12}O_6$). All three of these molecules are present in many kitchen recipes.

# States of Matter

Matter can change from one state to another, but water is still water as a solid (ice), liquid (water), or a gas (steam).

Atoms and molecules exist in different **states** depending on the environment. The three states of matter are solids, liquids, and gases. As a solid, matter maintains its own shape because its molecules stay very close together and vibrate, but not in a way you can see or feel. A slice of bread, a peanut, and a salt shaker are all examples of solids. Water is a liquid. As it cools, its molecules stop moving around freely and the water becomes solid as ice cubes. Ice left to melt changes from a solid state to a liquid as the water molecules start to move around more fluidly. Put water in a pot and boil it on a hot stove and it will turn into a gas. As water is heated to its boiling point, it begins to evaporate into steam. As a gas, **evaporated** water, or steam, molecules move quickly and spread out as far as they can. Salt and salt shakers are both solid matter.

## HOW WE KNOW

### Food Science

Humans require a good diet for health. Eating different types of food provides us with the **elements** found in nature that allow our bodies to properly function. An egg yolk, for example, has sulfur, sodium, and zinc, while cashews are a good source of the mineral magnesium. Milk and **tofu** both have calcium, while meat and spinach both have iron. Through eating a varied and well-balanced diet, you can get the trace elements required for a healthy life.

# Scientific Method

Scientists use a set of procedures to explore the world around them. These procedures are called scientific method and they involve observation, testing, and studying things to figure out how they work.

## Follow the Steps

In order for scientists to share information and ideas, they have to do things basically the same way. The scientific method helps them make sure that other scientists can repeat their experiments and results. Here are some steps for the scientific method:

1. Ask a question.
2. Research background information.
3. Construct a hypothesis (an explanation for how things function).
4. Create an experiment that tests the hypothesis.
5. Conduct the experiment.
6. Make observations and record results.
7. Figure out whether the results make the hypothesis true or false.

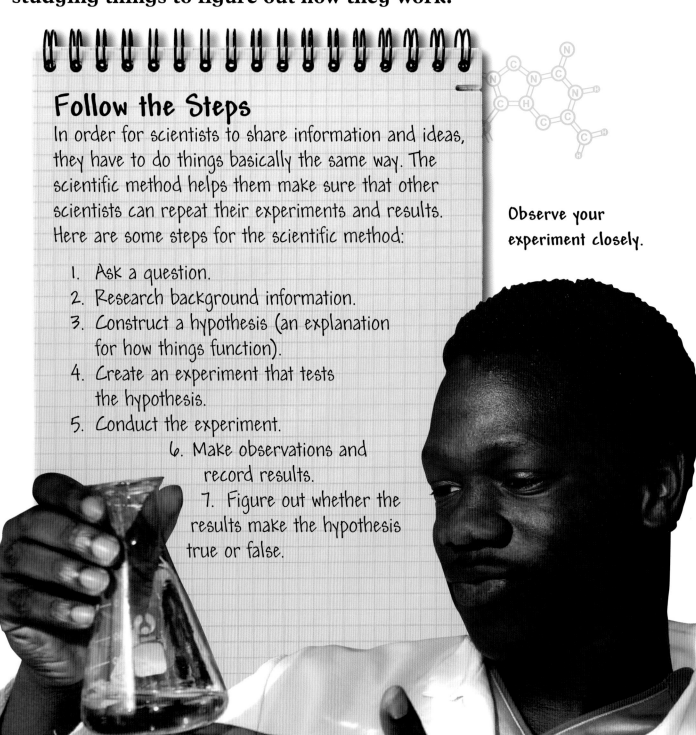

Observe your experiment closely.

# Asking Why

Scientists observe the world around them. They also ask questions about why things are the way they are. Scientists used to be kids too, and they asked questions like, "Why is the sky blue?" "Why does mold grow on old bread?" or "How do vegetables grow?" They listened to the answers given by their parents, teachers, and read books just like this one. Scientists still ask questions like these, but their questions are guided by the scientific method. They read and research their questions.

# What is a Hypothesis?

Scientists use hypotheses every day. A hypothesis is a prediction or educated guess that explains something. Scientists base their guesses on previous knowledge and other scientific facts. Using a hypothesis allows a scientist to make an experiment that tests their prediction. If they have guessed accurately, then their scientific results will show that what they guessed (the hypothesis) is true. Like everyone, scientists make guesses that are not correct. Sometimess they get things wrong. Their incorrect guesses help them to understand how to guess more accurately in the future. Some great discoveries have also been made through incorrect guessing.

Make notes for both your hypothesis and your conclusion.

# Good Observation

Baking a cake is a great way to learn how to observe. Once all the ingredients are poured in a pan and bound for a hot oven, you can begin observing. As you wait, the cake begins to cook and delicious smells drift through the room. These smells are carried by heated air that moves because its molecules are vibrating quickly. Go into another room and then as you walk back to the kitchen, notice when you smell the cake. Making observations of your environment is part of science. When scientists make observations, they record or write down what they see. Ask your mom or dad to turn on the light in the oven. Watch the surface of the cake. At first, it will seem wet, but then bubbles will appear on the surface. Also, watch how the surface texture changes as the cake hardens. Making an observation means paying close attention to what is happening. You can observe through all of your senses.

Cake ingredients are mixed in a specific order. Beating the batter incorporates air bubbles into the mixture, and air makes the final cake lighter.

# History and Method

The scientific method started a long time ago with ancient scientists. An early Greek scientist named Pythagoras used the scientific method to show that Earth is round. Over time, scientists made more rules for conducting experiments and presenting scientific results. The discoveries of many scientists, some famous and some not so famous, helped shape the scientific method into its modern form. For example, Nicolaus Copernicus (1473-1543) was a Polish astronomer who showed that Earth orbited the Sun. Italian astronomer Galileo Galilei (1564-1642) studied laws of motion, and Sir Isaac Newton (1642-1727) **formulated** the law of gravity.

Sir Isaac Newton was an English scientist who formulated the laws of gravity after observing an apple fall from a tree.

# HOW WE KNOW

## A Theory or a Law?

Science is based on both laws and theories. Laws are established rules for how things work and are accepted by almost all scientists. Although laws rarely change, sometimes new discoveries show that a law is wrong. A theory is a prediction about how things work. Some predictions are better than others. They help scientists see the world around them in a new way. Many accepted scientific laws started out as theories that very few people believed. For example, for centuries people believed that Earth was the center of the universe. Over time, theories showed that Earth orbited the Sun. Theories become laws through testing and experimentation.

# Chemistry of Life

The kitchen is the headquarters for chemical processes in the home. The fridge keeps food cold through cooling gases. Heat in the oven provides energy that increases the rate of many chemical reactions. Bubbles of carbon dioxide **gas cause bread, cake, and other baked goods to rise. Even the vitamins in vegetables are all part of chemistry.**

## Open Your Eyes

Next time you walk into the kitchen, use your new understanding of chemistry. Open the fridge. Besides the chemistry used to keep the inside cool, look for common chemicals and products. Milk is much more than a white liquid. In chemistry, it is known as an **emulsion** of milk-fats and water. Chemists also know that milk contains vitamins A, D, K, and E. As well, milk has a slightly sweet flavor because of lactose, a **carbohydrate** containing other simple sugars. Chemical reactions are constantly happening in the kitchen, whether we make them happen or not.

Milk is an emulsion because it contains fats and water.

## fun fact

Limonene is the essential oil in a lemon's peel that gives it a distinctly refreshing smell.

# Pancakes, Anyone?

Making pancakes is chemistry. Pancake batter is a **suspension**, or a fluid with small bits of solid flour floating in it. When pancake batter hits a hot pan, it sizzles. The heat from the pan provides energy that starts a chemical reaction. Baking powder, an ingredient used in pancake batter, contains sodium bicarbonate, cornstarch, and tartaric acid. When it combines with the moisture from milk and the heat from the pan, it creates a chemical reaction. Carbon dioxide is released and because it is lighter than the batter, it moves toward the surface. As the reaction increases, more bubbles are released. Gluten, an elastic and sticky substance from the flour, traps these bubbles as the batter becomes firm from cooking. After your pancake is flipped and cooked through, it will have changed from a suspension to a foam-like dough. The bubbles in your pancake are evidence of the chemical reaction.

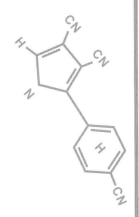

If you look closely, you can see the bubbles on a pancake while it is cooking. This is a chemical reaction.

# Chemistry in the Kitchen

If you watch cooks and bakers in a kitchen, you might notice something: bakers and cooks follow recipes. This is because, in kitchen science, baking and cooking require measuring, method, and timing.

When leavened, or risen, bread is made, flour is mixed with a liquid and yeast. A chemical reaction takes place when each of these ingredients are mixed together.

## Kitchen Reactions

A chemical reaction is what happens when two substances mix together and change each other's molecular structure, either by breaking bonds or making new ones. Professional bakers and chefs know that baking and cooking are applied chemistry. In the kitchen, making many different foods requires heat or motion to change the molecular bonds of ingredients, or mixtures.

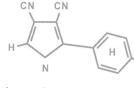

Making bread is also a process (much like all experiments are a process). At some point, the mixed dough must be kneaded. Kneading helps capture the carbon dioxide, the element that makes bread light and airy.

# Changing the Bonds

In chemistry, heat is known as thermal energy. Boiling or whipping, for example, can change weak hydrogen bonds. By adding small amounts of thermal energy, you can boil an egg or whip cream. The heat or thermal energy added in boiling or whipping causes the molecules to hit one another faster and more frequently. As this happens, the texture of the egg or the cream changes. Some bonds are very strong and require a higher degree of thermal energy to change. Frying an egg in a pan breaks down these bonds because it is a much hotter environment. This results in a browned texture and flavor. A chicken breast grilled on a barbecue tastes good because of the browning of the meat—or breaking of the bonds. Baking causes batter to change from a liquid suspension to a solid. All of these different textures and flavors are created by the addition of thermal energy or heat.

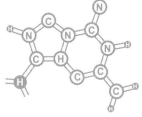

Adding heat, whether through beating or cooking, changes the bonds of a food.

## fun fact

Vinegar, or acetic acid, can cook foods by breaking down protein fibers. This is why it also makes an excellent marinate for tough meats.

# Fermentation and Yeast

Breads are divided into two categories: leavened and unleavened. Leavened breads are made using yeast as a rising agent. Unleavened breads are flatbreads like roti, chapati, or Matzah. Yeast is a fungi, like a mushroom, and it is alive. It can **ferment** the carbohydrates in flour by breaking the sugars down into carbon dioxide and alcohol. The carbon dioxide gathers in small bubbles in the dough, causing it to rise. The bubbles of carbon dioxide are held in place by gluten. When the dough has risen enough, it is baked in a hot oven. The hot air kills the yeast and hardens the dough around the bubbles. A slice of bread has texture because of the bubbles trapped in it. Next time you have a piece of leavened bread, look for the signs of yeast fermentation.

The bubbles in this bread are a sign of yeast fermentation.

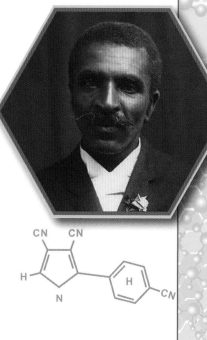

16

# HOW WE KNOW

## Cooking It Up

Cookware and bakeware are made of substances based on how they conduct heat. Pots and pans are typically used on top of the stove. Bakeware is ordinarily used in the oven. Pots and pans are usually made from metal compounds such as stainless steel or carbon steel. Single metals are not often used because they react with and change the flavor of foods at high heat. **Alloys** provide uniform heating surfaces and do not react with food easily.

## Sugars

Many people say they have a sweet tooth. What this means is that they like sugary food. Many favorite desserts and treats, such as brownies, cakes, cookies, candies, candy bars, and donuts, are made with sugar. To chemists, sugar refers to a family of chemical compounds. The one most commonly used in baking and cooking is sucrose. Sucrose is made from sugarcane and sugar beet plants. Other sugars like lactose, found in milk, and fructose, found in fruit and vegetables, are part of our diets as well. Sugars are a source of rapid energy.

## Fats

Fats have a bad reputation, but chemists and **nutritionists** know that some fats are good and some fats are not as healthy. Fats add flavor and texture to food in cooking. Ice cream just would not be ice cream without the fat naturally present in milk, its main ingredient. Ice cream also requires sugar, and sometimes eggs. These ingredients are churned, or mixed together, in a cold environment. This churning adds air, and the chemical reaction this creates results in both an emulsion and a foam.

Ice cream requires milk fat.

Sugar cane is a plant from which sugar is extracted.

# Testing Things

An experiment is a set of steps to test a hypothesis, or an assumption about how something works. A hypothesis can be simple or complex—but no matter the hypothesis, it requires testing.

## Experimenting

An experiment tests the hypothesis by producing results. When you are performing an experiment, you need to observe. Observations both during the experiment and after will prove a hypothesis true or false.

## Observing Things

Scientists repeat, or do experiments over and over again. This gives them many chances to observe what happens. When they see, hear, touch, or taste the results of the experiment, they are making observations. Observing an experiment requires focus and attention. What is happening may be obvious, but it could also be hard to detect. Scientists often use many special instruments in testing and observing. For example, there are microscopes for seeing very small objects, scales for measuring the mass of a substance, and other very sophisticated laboratory instruments.

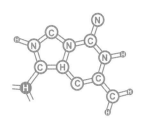

Observing requires that the experimenter pay attention to what is happening.

# Measuring the Results

Scientists use experiments to produce results. But what is a result? A result is a measurable phenomena, or something that can be detected. Chemists measure what happens in an experiment. They could weigh the mass of a material or the electricity produced through a chemical reaction. They may also measure the heat or thermal energy required to create an ideal reaction. Scientists also measure the volume of liquids and gases.

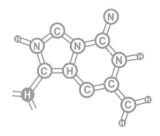

In a chemistry laboratory, chemists use equipment such as microscopes to help them observe experiments.

# Analyzing Results

After an experiment, a scientist has a set of observations and carefully measured results. What do they do next? Analysis is the next process. When scientists analyze results, they look for patterns, trends, or relationships. They try to figure out what the results mean. A big part of analysis is seeing whether the results prove the hypothesis true or false. By comparing the results, scientists are able to see patterns and decide whether the results are valid. Sometimes, scientists try to analyze the experimental results only to learn that the experiment did not work. Knowing when an experiment has not worked and understanding why it failed are important parts of science. Sometimes, failed experiments result in a serendipitous, or unexpected new discovery.

Scientists keep notes of their measurements and observations so they can analyze the data.

# Get Cracking!

**Can air change the texture of a food and improve how it tastes?**

**Question:** What makes a fluffy omelet?

**Hypothesis:** Air beaten into eggs can help them to rise when cooked.

## Materials:

2 eggs
2 teaspoons
(8 grams)
milk
(optional)

butter
bowl
whisk or fork
frying pan

## Method:

1. Crack two eggs into a bowl and add two teaspoons of milk.
2. Use the whisk and start beating vigorously for two minutes, and no more.
3. Ask an adult for help with the cooking. Melt some butter in a hot frying pan, then add the eggs. The volume of eggs and the pan diameter should be balanced.
4. Cook the eggs and then slide or flip one side of the omelet over on itself to finish cooking.

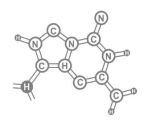

Crack the eggs in
a bowl.

Whisk or beat for
two minutes.

Fry the egg mixture in a
hot pan.

Observe and taste the results. Are the
eggs fluffy or rubbery?

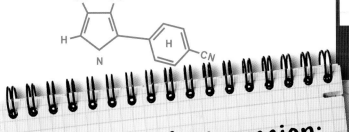

## Results and Discussion:

When you beat an egg, the whites and
the yolks form a mixture that has
some properties of both. Proteins in
the eggs unravel as air is whipped
into the eggs. Beat them too long
and the proteins completely unravel,
leaving you with rubbery eggs. The
air that is trapped in the partly
unraveled proteins keeps the eggs
light and fluffy when cooked.

How does cooking change the state
of the egg mixture?

# Biscuits Thick and Thin

**Everybody loves biscuits, but how do you make them light and flakey?**

Question:    How does baking soda work?

Hypothesis:  Biscuits made without baking soda will not rise.

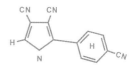

## Materials:

1 teaspoon (4 grams)
  baking soda
1/2 teaspoon
  (2 grams) salt
1 cup (228 grams)
  flour

2 tablespoons (28
  grams) butter
1/3 cup (82 ml) milk
1 baking sheet
2 mixing bowls
biscuit cutter or glass
rolling pin

## Method:

1. Preheat the oven to 450°F (230°C) and lightly grease the baking sheet.
2. In mixing bowl #1, place baking soda, flour, salt, and butter. Mix well. Then add milk.
3. In mixing bowl #2, repeat step 2, except DO NOT add baking soda.
4. Knead each pile of dough briefly, keeping them separate.
5. Use a rolling pin to flatten each pile out to a thickness of about a 1/2 inch (1.5 cm).
6. Cut out biscuits from each dough using the drinking glass or biscuit cutter. Place the biscuits from mixing bowl #1 on one end of the baking sheet, and those from mixing bowl #2 on the other.
7. Bake biscuits at 450°F (230°C) for 10-12 minutes.
8. Remove the biscuits and observe the differences. Try tasting a biscuit from each side. Record your observations.

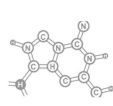

Use your hands to gently mix the butter into the flour mixture. Then mix in the milk.

Use the rolling pin to roll the dough to a thickness of about a 1/2 inch (1.5 cm) and cut biscuits out using a glass or the cutter.

When baked and cooled, examine your biscuits and make notes. Do they look and taste different?

## Results and Discussion:

The biscuits from mixing bowl #1 (with baking soda) will have risen, while those from mixing bowl #2 (without baking soda) will not have risen. When you tasted the risen biscuit, it was likely light and fluffy. The biscuit that did not rise was likely hard and chewy and it probably didn't taste that good.

Using what you learned about baking soda, explain why the first biscuit was fluffy, while the second was more like a hockey puck.

# Eureka! I Found It!

Moments of lucky insight or discovery happen in science. As a result, many great things have been understood and invented. A scientist may not have set out to discover a certain thing, but through luck, chance, and keen observations, a eureka moment happens.

## I Have Found It!

"Eureka!" is reportedly the word screamed by ancient Greek scientist Archimedes after he realized that the volume of water **displaced** in his bathtub was equal to the volume of his body. This chance observation helped Archimedes solve a scientific problem: finding a method for testing the purity of gold. This meant he could help his king test the honesty of his goldsmith by measuring his crown and the amount of water it displaced. Eureka is now the word many people exclaim when they discover something. There are many other examples of serendipitous "eurekas" in science.

Archimedes is said to have jumped out of the bath to run naked through the streets yelling "eureka," meaning "I have found it."

# Wrap It Up

Plastic wrap is used both in restaurants and at home to **preserve** food and make it portable. Before plastic wrap, people wrapped their sandwiches in paper or waxed paper, which did not hold together well. Plastic wrap was invented through a series of serendipitous discoveries at a Dow Chemical lab. In 1933, chemists Ralph Wiley was experimenting with a new dry cleaning product. As part of his experiment, he used many beakers. One beaker was coated with a substance that he could not remove. The substance called "eonite" was green, smelled bad, and was used as a spray on military aircraft to protect them. Wiley accidentally discovered PVDC (a kind of plastic) while cleaning his beakers. But PVDC did not become plastic wrap, or "saran wrap" as Dow called it, until the green color and bad smell were removed in 1953.

A sandwich in plastic wrap

# HOW WE KNOW

## Science of Onion Tears

Have your eyes ever watered when someone around you has been cutting raw onions? That's because onions, when they are chopped or damaged, produce a lacrimator, or a chemical substance that makes our eyes water. The tear-producing substance comes from the element sulphur, which the onion plant takes from the soil as it is growing. The plant uses it as a defense mechanism. When released by chopping, the substance escapes into the air and lands on our eyes and then breaks down into other irritating chemicals.

# The Sweet Stuff

Did you know that the artificial sweeteners saccharin and aspartame were discovered by accident? In 1878, while working on lab experiments with coal tar byproducts, chemist Constantin Falhberg discovered a substance that was sweet. Later, he named the no-calorie sweetener saccharin and it was used as a sugar replacement in prepared foods. Chemist James Schlatter discovered aspartame while working on chemical compounds that could help ulcers. He licked his fingers after working on the compound (something that could have been a poisonous chemtastrophe), and found it was sweet. Like saccharin, aspartame is used as a diet sugar replacement.

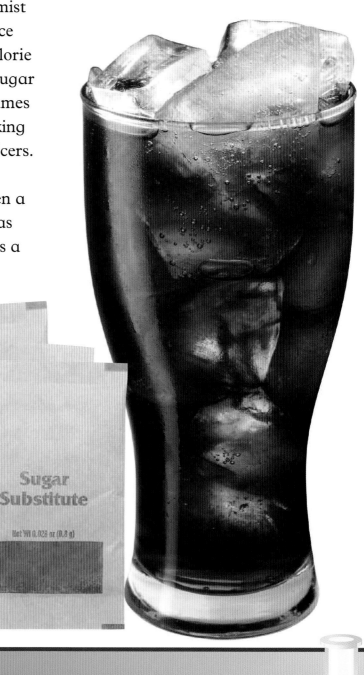

Sugar
Substitute

Net Wt 0.028 oz (0.8 g)

# fun fact

**Monosodium glutamate (MSG) is a flavor enhancer, or taste sensation, originally made from a form of seaweed.**

# Bread by Accident

The first breads were flat breads because ancient people had no way of making wheat dough rise. The first leavened, or risen, bread was a natural chemistry accident. Ancient bakers often left flat bread dough out before baking. Wild yeast floating in the air landed on the dough. Along with the yeast, there was a bacterial culture called lactobacillus. This culture worked in combination with the yeast and caused the bread to rise in a chemical reaction. Ancient bakers did not understand the chemical process that made their bread rise, but they saved a portion of risen dough and used it as the base for the next batch of bread dough. The lactobacillus, or lactic acid in the yeast, tastes slightly tangy and sour, so bread created through this process was called sourdough. Sourdough yeast cultures were the main form of leavened bread until around 1100 AD.

Some wheat was naturally colonized by wild yeast.

# HOW WE KNOW

## Asparagus and Stinky Urine

The vegetable asparagus has an unusual side effect that scientists say is due to a chemical reaction in human bodies. Many people notice that after eating asparagus, their urine has a skunky odor. **Biochemists** who have studied this say it is because human bodies turn asparagusic acid in the vegetable into methanethiol. Methanethiol is a close relative chemically to skunk spray. Some people do not produce this chemical after eating asparagus, and some do but cannot smell it.

# Creative Chemists

Chemistry is a huge field of study with many areas of specialization. Chemists examine everything from how a body digests food, to how drugs are made. Chemistry is a part of the everyday world, so it involves just about everything!

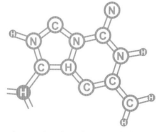

Good chefs and bakers must have a basic knowledge of chemistry.

## Cooks and Chemists

Just as chemists analyze substances to determine what is in them and what their properties are, bakers and chefs use chemistry to make and understand food. Knowing how an egg cooks allows a chef to make it just how the customer ordered. Understanding yeast or baking soda helps a baker make better breads, cakes, and pastries. Many food companies employ chemists to scientifically test their food. These food scientists try to make the best spaghetti sauce or best frozen dinner. By experimenting with different ingredients and processes, they create the meals you eat at home.

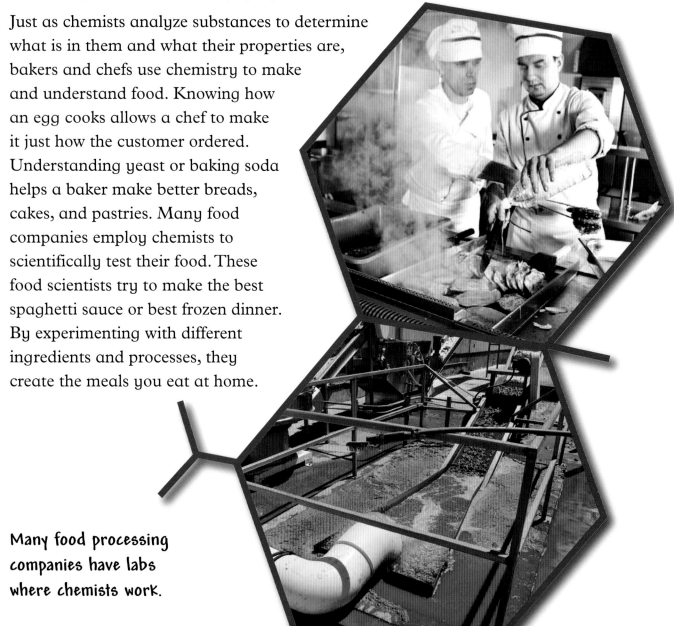

Many food processing companies have labs where chemists work.

# What is Molecular Gastronomy?

Molecular gastronomy is the chemistry, biology, and **physics** behind cooking. It is also a new area of scientific study that looks at the physical and chemical processes and changes that happen in cooking. Molecular gastronomers use the tools and methods of science labs to investigate cooking and find new ways to make food. Some of the world's most famous and inventive chefs practice molecular gastronomy. They often create new foods and flavors such as foamy whipped egg whites that are specially cooked to become jelly, vapors that taste like beets or bacon, and edible menus that taste like steak and are made from potato starch.

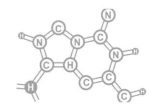

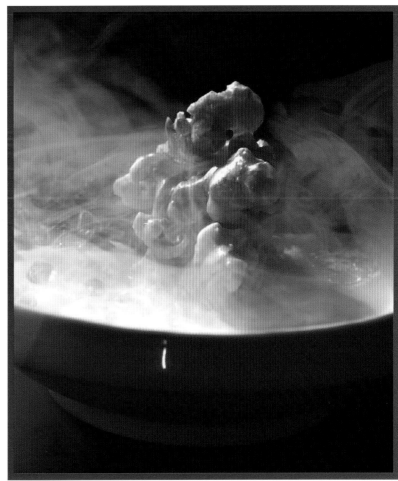

This molecular gastronomy dessert is a caramel popcorn vanilla panna cotta flash-frozen with liquid nitrogen. Liquid nitrogen is a fluid that rapidly freezes things. Nitrogen is a chemical element that is usually a gas.

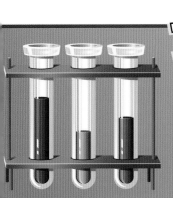

# fun fact

"Today, you've got bakers working to find the best flour, the best yeast, the best oven. This is science, pure and simple. But people still say they're shocked if science participates in cooking."
-Ferran Adria, famous chef and molecular gastronomist

# Want to Learn More?

**Dreaming of becoming a chemist, chef, or food scientist? Well, here are some resources and places to learn about the amazing science of chemistry and how it relates to the kitchen.**

## Chemistry Websites:

### Rader's Chem4Kids!
**www.chem4kids.com**
A fascinating website that offers an introductory perspective on chemical concepts like atoms, molecules, reactions, and much more. Games and quizzes are also available on the site.

### Strange Matter
**www.strangematterexhibit.com/index.html**
An exciting and interactive website that looks at chemical concepts through material science. With both educational videos and fun games, there is something for everyone here.

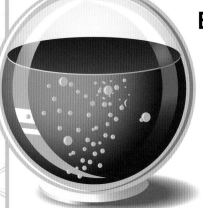

### The Open Door Website: Chemistry
**www.saburchill.com/chemistry/visual/PT/001.html**
This resource provides an interactive version of the periodic table. By clicking on an element, you can learn a lot about the structure, function, and uses of that atom.

### BrainPop
**www.brainpop.com/science/matterandchemistry/**
Find answers to all your chemistry questions! This interactive site makes learning fun with the help of games, videos, and fascinating animations.

# Chemistry Books:

**Why Chemistry Matters** series. Crabtree Publishing, 2009. This series uses common examples from everyday life to help explain basic chemistry.

**Chemistry** by Dr. Anne Newmark: Dorling Kindersley, 2000. This book has ample and varied information on topics in chemistry, which are presented both thematically and historically.

**Step into Science** series. Crabtree Publishing, 2010. Each book in this series explores a step in the scientific method.

**Science Fun at Home** by Chris Maynard: Dorling Kindersley, 2006. This fun book has more than 100 experiments that you can perform at school or at home.

**Cool Chemistry Concoctions: 50 Formulas that Fizz, Foam, Splatter & Ooze** by Joe Rhatigan, Veronika Gunter, and Tom La Baff: Larch Books, 2007. Another book of fun household experiments.

# Places to Learn More:

### American Museum of Science and Energy
**Oak Ridge, Tennessee**

Focused on the science of energy, the AMSE is a great place to discover the chemistry involved in energy production.

### Detroit Science Center
**Detroit, Michigan**

This science center offers a wide range of interactive exhibits for kids of all ages. From the chemistry of the steel industry to the chemistry of life, many innovative programs exist for children.

### Lawrence Hall of Science
**Berkeley, California**

This research museum offers full programming for K-12 students with interactive exhibits and science camps. With ample opportunities for educational experiences and experimentation, this is a museum not to be missed.

# Glossary

**alloys** Mixed metals

**bond** Something that joins, ties, or fastens together

**carbohydrate** A compound in some foods that is rich in energy. Sugars and starches are carbohydrates

**carbon dioxide** A gas without color or odor that is made up of carbon and oxygen

**displaced** To move out of the usual or proper place

**elements** Any of the 107 substances that cannot be separated into simpler substances by using chemistry

**emulsion** A mixture consisting of drops of one liquid suspended in another liquid that does not mix well with the first

**evaporated** To turn from liquid into gas

**ferment** A chemical change or breakdown caused by yeasts or bacteria

**formulated** To devise, invent, or develop in a clear or methodical way

**knead** Press and mix with your hands

**mass** The amount of matter something contains

**nutritionists** One who is trained or is an expert in the study of foods and their health value

**particles** A tiny division of matter

**philosopher** One who studies the nature of life, truth, knowledge, and other important human matters

**physics** The science that deals with matter and energy, their qualities, and the relationships between them

**preserve** To keep or save from decomposition or rotting

**reactions** A chemical process where two substances are changed into another

**states** The physical condition of a substance

**suspension** A chemical mixture in which particles are not dissolved in a fluid

**texture** The feel or look of a substance

**tofu** A food made from soybean milk that looks and feels like soft cheese.

# Index